A WORSHIP ANTHOLOGY
FOR ADVENT
& CHRISTMAS

Readings, Poems and Collects

compiled by
H.J.RICHARDS

Kevin
Mayhew

First published in 1994 by
KEVIN MAYHEW LTD
Rattlesden
Bury St Edmunds
Suffolk IP30 0SZ

ISBN 0 86209 565 4
Catalogue No 1500013

Front cover: *Nativity* (detail) from nave window
by C. E. Kempe (1890), All Saints' Church, Cambridge.
Reproduced by kind permission of Woodmansterne Picture
Library and Derrick Witty.

Cover design by Juliette Clarke and Graham Johnstone
Typesetting and Page Creation by Vicky Allwork-Brown
Printed and bound in Great Britain.

CONTENTS

Contents

FOREWORD

This anthology has been put together to provide resource
material for services during the Advent and Christmas
season. It contains a number of newly translated biblical
texts, and a selection of readings, meditations, poems and
prayers drawn from different countries, centuries and
, from which a number of different services can
cted.

ians would vote Advent and Christmas their
e of the year. They know it does not have the
ical or liturgical status as Easter, but there is a
d warmth about it which inspires them more
season. Most compelling is its ability to
believe world to which Christ has not yet
hen his birth is finally announced, it is as if
man history had taken place in their midst.

e' is the wrong word. Merely to recollect
o re-present it is actually to bring it into
is the very purpose of ritual and liturgy: to
make the past, which could easily die on us, remain ever
alive and ever new. Through our celebration of Advent and
Christmas, God answers our yearning for the Messiah to
come, and Christ is born in very truth in our midst, over
and over again.

H. J. RICHARDS

1 WAITING

Scripture Readings

The time will come
when all the nations of the earth
will beat their swords into ploughshares
and their spears into sickles.
No nation will any longer fight against another
because no one will teach them how.

A new branch will grow out of the tree which bore David,
a new shoot coming out of the same root.
He will live his life in the very Spirit of God,
a Spirit of wisdom, insight, heroism and reverence . . .
He will stand up for the poor and the needy,
justice the belt around his waist,
and dependability the cloak round his shoulders.

The wolf will lie down together with the lamb,
the panther will nestle down beside the goat,
calf and lion will graze on the same field,
a child leading both of them to pasture . . .
Infants will play beside the adder's nest,
and children put their hands safely into the snake's den . . .
As the sea floor is covered with water
the whole earth will be covered with peace.

If only you would tear the heavens apart and come down,
shaking the mountains as you descend,
and setting the forests alight,
convincing the doubters that you exist,
and making all the nations catch their breath! . . .
No ear has heard, no eye has seen
the wonders you will do
for those who believe in you.

BOOK OF ISAIAH 2:4, 11:1-9, 64:1-4

O Come, Emmanuel

O come , O come, Emmanuel,
and ransom captive Israel,
that mourns in lonely exile here
until the Son of God appear.
    Rejoice! Rejoice! Emmanuel
    shall come to thee, O Israel.

O come, thou Rod of Jesse, free
thine own from Satan's tyranny;
from depth of hell thy people save,
and give them victory o'er the grave.

O come, thou Dayspring, come and cheer
our spirits by thine advent here;
disperse the gloomy clouds of night,
and death's dark shadows put to flight.

O come, O come, thou Lord of might,
who to thy tribes, on Sinai's height,
in ancient times didst give the law
in cloud, and majesty, and awe.

O come, thou Key of David, come,
and open wide our heavenly home;
make safe the way that leads on high,
and close the path to misery.
    Rejoice! Rejoice! Emmanuel
    shall come to thee, O Israel.

'O ANTIPHONS', (12TH-13TH CENTURY),
TRS. JOHN MASON NEALE (1818-1866)

Thy Kingdom Come

Lord our God, we put our hope in you.
Soon let us witness the glory of your power;
when the worship of material things shall pass away from the earth,
and prejudice and superstition shall at last be cut off;
when the world will be set right by the rule of God,
and all mankind shall speak out in your name,
and all the wicked of the earth shall turn to you.
Then all who inhabit this world shall meet in understanding,
and shall know that to you alone each one shall submit,
and pledge himself in every tongue.
In your presence, Lord our God,
they shall bow down and be humble,
honouring the glory of your being.
All shall accept the duty of building your Kingdom,
so that your reign of goodness shall come soon and last forever.
For yours alone is the true Kingdom,
and only the glory of your rule endures forever.

JEWISH SABBATH EVENING PRAYER

Come, Lord Jesus

Come to us, Lord Jesus Christ,
come as we search the scriptures and see God's hidden purpose,
come as we walk the lonely road, needing a companion,
come when life mystifies and perplexes us,
come into our disappointments and unease,
come at table when we share our food and hopes,
and, coming, open our eyes to recognise you.

DONALD HILTON (B. 1932)

Come, Radiant Sun

Hail, heavenly beam, brightest of angels thou,
sent unto men upon this middle-earth!
Thou are the true refulgence of the sun,
radiant above the stars, and from thyself
illuminest for ever all the tides of time.
And as thou, God indeed begotten of God,
thou Son of the true Father, wast from aye,
without beginning, in the heaven's glory,
so now thy handiwork in its sore need
prayeth thee boldly that thou send to us
the radiant sun, and that thou comest thyself
to enlighten those who for so long a time
were wrapt around with darkness, and here in gloom
have sat the livelong night, shrouded in sin.

CYNEWULF, BISHOP OF LINDISFARNE (8TH CENTURY).

This Is What Advent Is

Advent should admonish us to discover
in each brother or sister that we greet,
in each friend whose hand we shake,
in each beggar who asks for bread,
in each worker who wants to use the right to join a union,
in each peasant who looks for work in the coffee groves,
the face of Christ.

Then it would not be possible to rob them,
to cheat them,
to deny them their rights.

They are Christ,
and whatever is done to them
Christ will take as done to him.
This is what Advent is:
Christ living among us.

OSCAR ROMERO (1917-1980)

The Messiah Comes

How beautiful on the mountains
are the banners of the herald
who come proclaiming peace!
He brings joyful news
that salvation is at hand
and says to Zion:
Your God reigns!

Rejoice, then, and behold the King!
The Messiah comes!
He is righteous and victorious
yet in humility he rides on an ass's foal.

The Lord says:
See! I send you a messenger
to prepare the way for me!
And immediately,
after so much wandering, so much seeking,
there will appear to you the shining vision
of the Lord in his temple:
it is the Angel of the Covenant,
the Lord of hosts!
He says to you: Behold,
before the great and terrible Day of the Lord
I will send you again
the prophet Elijah;
he reconciles the hearts of fathers to their sons
and the hearts of sons to their fathers,
that my coming shall not be one of sorrow but of joy.

The days are coming, says the almighty Lord,
when the Shoot of David will be among you,
and then he who is the true King
will reign with great wisdom,
righteousness and compassion.
See, in those days
Judah will be saved
and Israel live.

JEWISH SABBATH AFTERNOON PRAYER

Till He Comes

What a joy for us to praise you,
Lord God, our Father,
in this season of expectation!
For, throughout human history,
the road that cannot lead astray
is being readied –
full of sharp turns,
but equally full of wonders;
full of darkness,
yet suddenly kind.
Everything has paved the way for Christ,
whom we herald till he comes.

That is why,
with the whole world
that is moving towards the Kingdom,
but likewise with all the prophets
and the impatient,
with people of faith and hope
and those who hunger for justice and peace,
we sing the hymn of your glory –
the hymn of the new heavens
and the new earth:

Holy, holy, holy, Lord God of power and might;
heaven and earth are full of your glory;
Hosanna in the highest.
Blessed in the name of the Lord is he who comes.
Hosanna in the highest.

PIERRE GRIOLET

The Spirit of Wonder

There are several attitudes towards Christmas,
Some of which we may disregard:
The social, the torpid, the patently commercial,
The rowdy (the pubs being open till midnight),
And the childish – which is not that of the child
For whom the candle is a star, and the gilded angel
Spreading its wings at the summit of the tree
Is not only a decoration, but an angel.
The child wonders at the Christmas Tree:
Let him continue in the spirit of wonder
At the Feast as an event, not accepted as a pretext;
So that the glittering rapture, the amazement
Of the first-remembered Christmas Tree,
So that the surprises, delight in new possessions
(Each one with its peculiar and exciting smell),
The expectation of the goose or turkey
And the expected awe on its appearance,
So that the reverence and the gaiety
May not be forgotten in later experience,
In the bored habituation, the fatigue, the tedium,
The awareness of death, the consciousness of failure,
Or in the piety of the convert
Which may be tainted with a self-conceit
Displeasing to God and disrespectful to the children
(And here I remember also with gratitude
St. Lucy, her carol, and her crown of fire):
So that before the end, the eightieth Christmas
(By 'eightieth' meaning whichever is the last)
The accumulated memories of annual emotion
May be concentrated into a great joy
Which shall also be a great fear, as on the occasion
When fear came upon every soul:
Because the beginning shall remind us of the end
And the first coming of the second coming.

THE CULTIVATION OF CHRISTMAS TREES BY T. S. ELIOT (1888-1965)

Trembling Expectancy

Art thou a stranger to my country, Lord?
My land of black roots and thick jungles
where the wild boar sharpens his tusks,
and the monkeys chatter in the trees,
and the peacock's shrill note
echoes through the mist-clad hills;

my land of brown, caked river mud
where the elephant and the leopard come to drink,
and the shambling bear with his dreamy eyes
sees the porcupine shedding his quills;

my land with its friezes of palmyra palms
etched sharply against the blue mountains;

my land of low-lying plains
with its miles of murmuring paddy fields
that stretch in undulating waves of green
to the distant horizon;

my land of sapphire skies and flaming sunsets,
my land of leaden grey skies piled high
with banks of monsoon clouds;

my land of stinging rain and burning heat,
of dark nights, of enchanting moons
that dance behind the coconut fronds;

my land of tanks and pools
where the lazy buffalo wallows
and the red lotuses lie asleep?

Nay, thou art no stranger, Lord,
for the wind whispers of thee
and the waters chant thy name.
The whole land is hushed in trembling expectancy,
awaiting thy touch of creative Love.

CHANDRAN DEVANESEN

In Thy Coming

Let me love thee, O Christ,
in thy first coming,
when thou wast made man, for love of men,
and for love of me.

Let me love thee, O Christ,
in thy second coming,
when with an inconceivable love
thou standest and knockest at the door,
and wouldest enter into the souls of men,
and into mine.

Plant in my soul, O Christ,
thy likeness of love,
that when by death thou callest,
it may be ready
and burning
to come unto thee.

ERIC MILNER-WHITE

A New Future

When King Herod heard this, he was perturbed
and so was the whole of Jerusalem. (*Matthew* 2:3)

Herod had a right to be perturbed.
So does every Herod who sits on a throne of his people's bones,
and drinks his people's tears as unrighteous wine.

For coming to birth in Bethlehem
is a new Future for those on the margins of power.
The old arrangement will be no more,
and the One who whispered in Abraham's ear
and flared in Moses' face
will once more pull down the mighty from their thrones.
The baby's helplessness will prove stronger,
and Herod will be declared NO-KING.

The madonna's smile signifies something
only understood in Israel's blood:
soon the hungry will be filled with good things.
Scream, rage and weep – 'no-kings', wherever you sit:
El Salvador, Guatemala, Pretoria, Moscow, Washington,
Downing Street.
Jesus comes,
and through us will build
God's Kingdom of peace and justice.

TED SCHMIDT (B. 1939)

Liberty for Captives

We wait for something, someone
to light our twentieth century night of death,
to redeem the seventy eight million who died
to keep the world a safer place for democracy
(and profit and control).

We wait for the birth of the one
who will stay the final anointing of cinder and ash,
who will make it all new,
transform our lives,
heal our necrophilia.

We can no longer abide the official optimism
of those who invoke the bigger pie.
There are no tears here, nothing of solidarity or hope,
no understanding of the view from the edge.
There is no realisation that the Kingdom-bringer
waits in the virgin womb, ripe
to burst forth with liberty for the captives.

It is rumoured that thrones will be upended,
and every Caesar stands on a banana skin.
Christos, the Holy One of God, will never
bless the silos, wear the military tunic,
or sanctify the Empire.

He will offer a new heaven and a new earth,
and to toast his Christmas arrival,
you must also dance at his Friday coronation.

Emmanuel, come warm our global stable
with Spirit fire.

TED SCHMIDT (B. 1939)

Today I am Coming

Rabbi Joshua came upon the prophet Elijah as he was standing at the entrance of a cave. He asked him, 'When is the Messiah coming?'

He replied, 'Go and ask him yourself.'

'Where shall I find him?'

'Before the gates of Rome.'

'By what sign shall I know him?'

'He is sitting among the poor people, covered with wounds . . .'

So he went and found him, and said, 'Peace be with you, my master and teacher!'

He replied, 'Peace be with you, son of Levi!'

Then he asked him, 'When are you coming, master?'

He replied, 'Today!'

Rabbi Joshua returned to Elijah and told him, 'He has deceived me, deceived me! He told me, "Today I am coming!" and he has not come.'

Elijah said, 'What he told you was, "Today" – *if you would only hear his voice'. (Psalm 95:7)*

FROM THE TALMUD, MISHNAH SANHEDRIN

The Appearing of the Saviour

O gladsome light, O grace
of God the Father's face,
the eternal splendour wearing;
celestial, holy, blest,
our Saviour Jesus Christ,
joyful in thine appearing.

Now, ere day fadeth quite,
we see the evening light,
our wonted hymn outpouring;
Father of might unknown,
thee, his incarnate Son,
and Holy Spirit adoring.

To thee of right belongs
all praise of holy songs,
O Son of God, Lifegiver;
thee, therefore, O Most High,
the world doth glorify,
and shall exalt for ever.

ORTHODOX NIGHT PRAYER 'PHOS HILARON'
TRS. ROBERT BRIDGES (1844-1931)

It Will All Come Right

The difficulty in these times is that ideals, dreams and cherished hopes rise within us, only to meet the horrible truth and be shattered. It's really a wonder that I haven't dropped all my ideals, because they seem so absurd and impossible to carry out. Yet I keep them, because in spite of everything I still believe that people are really good at heart. I simply can't build up my hopes on a foundation consisting of confusion, misery and death. I see the world gradually being turned into a wilderness, I hear the ever-approaching thunder, which will destroy us too, I can feel the suffering of millions.

And yet, if I look up into the heavens, I think that it will all come right, that this cruelty too will end, and that peace and tranquillity will return again.

In the meantime, I must uphold my ideals, for perhaps the time will come when I shall be able to carry them out.

ANNE FRANK (1929-1945),
DIARY 15 JULY, 1944

The God Who Comes

Lord God, we adore you because you have come to us in the past.
You have spoken to us in the Law of Israel.
You have challenged us in the words of the Prophets.
You have shown us in Jesus what you are really like.

Lord God, we adore you because you still come to us now.
You come to us through other people and their love and concern for us,
You come to us through men and women who need our help.
You come to us as we worship you with your people.

Lord God, we adore you because you will come to us at the end.
You will be with us at the hour of death.
You will still reign supreme when all human institutions fail.
You will still be God when our history has run its course.

We welcome you, the God who comes.
Come to us now in the power of Jesus Christ our Lord.

ANON

2 MARY

Scripture Readings

Shout for joy, Jerusalem,
for I am coming to dwell with you,
says the Lord.

THE PROPHET ZECHARIAH 2:14

Shout for joy, Jerusalem,
the Lord, the King of Israel,
is in your midst:
you have nothing more to fear.
The Lord your God is in your midst.
He comes as a Saviour,
to rejoice in you with song,
to renew you in his love,
to dance with you in joy.

THE PROPHET ZEPHANIAH 3:14-17

Do not be afraid, be glad and rejoice,
for the Lord has worked marvels.
Jerusalem, rejoice in the Lord your God.

THE PROPHET JOEL 2:21-23

God sent his angel
to the town of Nazareth in Galilee,
to a young woman called Mary
who was engaged to a man called Joseph,
a distant descendant
of king David.
The angel said to her,
'Shout for joy, Mary,
beloved of God!
The Lord is in your midst.'
Mary was startled, and wondered
what these words could mean.
The angel said,
'Do not be afraid, Mary.
God has chosen you
to be the mother of his Son.
You must give the baby
the name "Jesus",
which means
"God has come as our Saviour".
He will inherit the throne
of his ancestor David,
and rule over God's people for ever.'
Mary said,
'How can this come about?
I am not yet married.'
The angel replied,
'The power of God will enfold you.
Nothing is impossible for God.'
Mary said,
'I am here to serve the Lord.
Let it be as you have said.
The Almighty
has worked this marvel for me.'

GOSPEL OF LUKE 1:26-49

The Slave of the Lord

Father, I thank you for what you have revealed of yourself
    in Mary's virgin-motherhood.
She was humble so you exalted her;
she was poor so you enriched her;
she was empty so you filled her;
she was your servant so you cared for her;
she had no future, by reason of her virginity,
    so you brought to birth in her
    the world's future, Jesus Christ our Lord.
Mary responded to your message
    with faith and love.
Behold, she said, the slave of the Lord;
let the Lord's Word be fulfilled in me.

Lord, through Mary's faith and love and humble service,
    your Word was made flesh
    and dwelt among us.
You exalted Mary your slave
    who humbled herself in her virginity
as you were to exalt your slave Jesus
    when he humbled himself
    even to the death of the cross.

Father, I pray that through the Virgin Mary
    I may learn what you expect of me.
May I become, through grace, humble and poor,
    empty and a slave,
so that you may exalt and enrich me,
so that you may fill me with heavenly blessings
    and bring Christ to birth
    through faith in my heart.

PETER DE ROSA (B. 1932)

Jewish Madonna

From the moment they were engaged
she looked at her man, remembering
the command to be fruitful,
and wondered what it would be like
making a child with Joseph
who was good with his hands.
She had not reckoned on the Angel,
but she did not laugh at all,
not like some when good news came,
strange conceptions, out of the blue,
of impossible children.

In the months to come she wished,
whilst shelling the peas,
that her body could pop like a pod,
and God could make childbirth easy.
She'd heard the cries of women being delivered
as if they were undergoing a crucifixion.
But when it began, her waters broke with his name
and she clenched her teeth on his name,
when his head was crowned.
She felt glad at the birth of her son
under a star, of David's line.
Except when the gifts appeared.

She could swear that he focused his eyes
in a way too early for babies.
When his hand touched the coffer of myrrh
he cried, as if something was pricking his palm.
He wrinkled his nose at her
when the incense was laid at his feet
unlit in its silver boat,
as if he sensed smoke, acrid and wrong,
like a paschal lamb left too long on the fire,
like a holocaust.
And the glint of the magi's gold.
seemed to appal him;
his inarticulate fist went to his mouth
as if an imagined tooth troubled his mind.

Later, she said that he came
with the look of someone who'd seen
a black hole at the heart of the world
before he entered her womb,
and that she wished she had disobeyed
the imperative Angel,
not trusted the span of his wings;
for a minute, that is,
until she put the child to her breast.
He knew how to suck like a lamb
with all the vigour of Spring.

NADINE BRUMMER

A Dissenter's Hail Mary

You bore him, fed him, clothed him, led him;
you carried him, suckled him, sang him to sleep.
You nursed him, enfolded him, encouraged him, scolded him;
you suffered him, moved him to laugh (and to weep).
You were the chosen one, you were the maiden,
he was yours before he was ours.
With your flesh the Word was laden,
Seed of eternity, Hope of the years.
For your obedience, your faith and your firmness,
for your humility, tenderness, grace,
sinners salute you: presume to say 'Thank you',
who love him and serve him
but had not your place.

JAMES BADCOCK (B. 1915)

Hail Mary

Our Father in heaven,
we join the angel in saying, 'Hail Mary'.

She is the beginning of the good news
that Jesus comes to us.
You chose her and loved her
to show us how chosen and loved all of us are.

How blessed is the mother who gave birth to that child,
and how blessed is the child she gave birth to,
through whom we know exactly what you are like.

We hold her hand as we ask you to accept us,
now, and at the testing time of our death. Amen.

THE PRAYER 'HAIL MARY'
TRS. H. J. RICHARDS (B. 1921)

Godes Mother

I sing of a maiden that is matchless;
King of all kings for her son she ches (chose).

He came all so still where his mother was,
as dew in April that falleth on the grass.

He came all so still to his mother's bowr,
as dew in April that falleth on the flower.

He came all so still where his Mother lay,
as dew in April that falleth on the spray.

Mother and maiden was never none but she;
well may such a lady Godes mother be.

ANON

I Carry the Maker of the World

Come, love, carolling along in me!
Come, love, carolling along in me!
All the while, wherever I may be,
I carry the maker of the world in me.

Lifting and loving you that I am not,
though your body is my bone and blood,
I wonder at the maker who can be
before I am and yet a child of me.

I lift and I carry you to Bethlehem,
I lift and I carry you to Galilee;
I'll carry you wherever I may be,
I carry the maker of the world in me.

In the beginning you were there, I know,
and you will carry me wherever I go.
I'll carry you wherever I may be,
I carry the maker of the world in me.

SYDNEY CARTER (B. 1915)

Blessed Among Women

Mary the slum-dweller
Mary who longed for the liberation of her people
Mary who sang to God of the poor
Mary homeless in Bethlehem
Mother of the longed-for Saviour
Mary exiled from her native land
Mary pilgrim with her people
Blessed are you among women.

FROM NOTICIAS ALIADAS

Virgin Mother

Maiden, yet a mother,
daughter of thy Son,
high beyond all other,
lowlier is none;
thou the consummation
planned by God's decree,
when our lost creation
nobler rose in thee.

Thus his place prepared,
he who all things made
'mid his creatures tarried,
in thy bosom laid;
there his love he nourished,
warmth that gave increase
to the root whence flourished
our eternal peace.

Lady, lest our vision,
striving heavenward, fail,
still let thy petition
with thy Son prevail,
unto whom all merit,
power and majesty
with the Holy Spirit
and the Father be.

DANTE ALIGHIERI (1265-1321)
TRS. R. A. KNOX (1888-1957)

Full of Grace

Of the Father's love begotten,
ere the worlds began to be,
he is Alpha and Omega,
he the source, the ending he,
of all things that are and have been
and that future years shall see:
evermore and evermore.

By his word was all created;
he commanded, it was done:
heav'n and earth and depth of ocean,
universe of three in one,
all that grows beneath the shining
of the light of moon and sun:
evermore and evermore.

Blessed was that day for ever,
when the Virgin, full of grace,
by the Spirit's pow'r conceiving,
bore the Saviour of our race;
and the child, the world's Redeemer,
first revealed his sacred face:
evermore and evermore.

AURELIUS PRUDENTIUS (348-405)
TRS. J. M. NEALE (1818-1866) ET AL.

Motherhood

Mary used to take hold of his hand
and lead him along the roads, saying,
'My sweet son, walk a little',
just as all other babies are taught to walk.
And he, Jesus, God himself,
happily followed her.
He clung to her with his little fingers,
stopping from time to time,
and hanging on to the skirts of his mother Mary,
he on whom the whole universe depends.
He would look up into her face,
and she would catch him up to her breast,
and walk along with him in her arms.

SERMON OF ST CYRIL OF ALEXANDRIA, 5TH CENT.

Queen of Heaven

Hail, O Queen of heaven enthroned!
Hail, by angels mistress owned,
Root of Jesse! Gate of morn!
Whence the world's true light was born.
Glorious Virgin, joy to thee,
Loveliest whom in heaven they see.
Fairest thou, where all are fair!
Plead with Christ our sins to spare.

AVE REGINA COELORUM

3 A Son is Born

Scripture Readings

Time was when Galilee was humbled by invaders;
the time will come when its glory will be restored.
A people that dwelt in darkness will see a great light;
on those who were overshadowed by death, light will shine again.

You have given new heart to this people, O God,
and they rejoice as people do at harvest time,
as victors do when they share the spoils;
for you have broken the yoke that crushed them
and the tyrant's rod that oppressed them,
as you did when Gideon overthrew the Midianites.
All the heavy army-boots and bloodstained uniforms
will now feed the flames and be burnt.

For a child has been born for us, a son given to us,
and he shall be robed in the royal purple,
and these titles conferred on him:
'Wonderful Counsellor, Mighty God,
Eternal Father, Prince of Peace.'

THE PROPHET ISAIAH 9:1-6

At this time, the Roman Emperor Augustus
ordered that a census should be made
of the whole Roman Empire.
Everyone had to be registered
in the town where his family came from.
So Joseph set out from Nazareth in Galilee
to go to Bethlehem in Judaea,
the hometown of descendants of David,
so that he could register there
with his fiancée Mary, who was pregnant.
While they were in Bethlehem,
the time came for Mary to have her baby.
It was a boy, her first.
She wrapped him in a blanket
and laid him in a manger,
the animals' feeding trough,
because there was no room for them in the house.

GOSPEL OF LUKE 2:1-7

I Sing the Birth

I sing the birth was born tonight,
the Author both of life and light,
the angels so did sound it:
and like the ravished shepherds said,
who saw the light and were afraid,
yet searched, and true they found it.
The Son of God, the eternal King,
that did us all salvation bring,
and freed the soul from danger;
he whom the whole world could not take,
the Word which heaven and earth did make,
was now laid in a manger.

The Father's wisdom willed it so,
the Son's obedience knew no No,
both wills were one in stature:
and as that wisdom hath decreed,
the Word was now made flesh indeed,
and took on him our nature.
What comfort by him do we win,
who made himself the price of sin,
to make us heirs of glory!
To see this Babe, all innocence,
a martyr born in our defence –
can man forget this story?

BEN JONSON (1573-1637)

God So Loved

What is the use of words?
Consider these
(we've heard them many, many times):
that 'God' so 'loved' the world
that he 'gave' his 'only-begotten Son',
that whoso 'believeth in him'
shall have 'everlasting life'.
These words hold truth.
These words are quite inadequate.
These words are almost inaccessible.
But these are all we have.

W. S. Beattie

Lord of Surprises

Lord Jesus Christ,
you came to a stable
when men looked in a palace;
you were born in poverty
when we might have anticipated riches;
King of all the earth,
you were content to visit one nation.
From beginning to end
you upturned our human values
and held us in suspense.
Come to us, Lord Jesus.
Do not let us take you for granted
or pretend that we ever fully understand you.
Continue to surprise us
so that, kept alert,
we are always ready
to receive you as Lord and to do your will.

Donald Hilton (b. 1932)

The Unspeakable New

When the angels had gone from them into heaven,
the shepherds said, 'Let us go to Bethlehem
to see this thing that has happened' *(Luke 2:15).*

Luke's story still jolts.
What he says is this:
The first people to gaze upon Novelty,
to see another Chance in a world grown weary –
were the niggers of religious Palestine,
Jews who worked the midnight shift
and so could not observe the Mosaic laws!

Isn't it ironic, delightful?
Jewish humour, even then:
shepherds, losers, forgotten ones,
unable to keep dietary laws
or attend the synagogue,
poor men, invisible to Rome,
forgotten by Jerusalem,
waiting
waiting
ready to be summoned, called to themselves.

Priest, Levite, Pharisee, Sadducee, Roman: all blind,
all imposing limited vision on a grace-filled universe.
The shepherd first sees.

Are we ready for the unspeakable New?
Or are we resigned to the weary, the worn out,
locked into a determined cosmos
where there are no surprises?
We believe Novelty comes, always comes,
breaking us, remaking us.
Are we ready? Fine.
Let us go to Bethlehem to see this thing that has happened.

TED SCHMIDT (B. 1939)

Your Child Jesus

We thank you, God our Father:
you have revealed to us your love,
you have told us the secret of Life,
in your Child, Jesus.

We give you thanks, our Father:
you, whose name is holy,
have visited and hallowed us
through your Child, Jesus.

Praise to you for creating the universe
so that the human race
can find food and drink;
but you have given us the food of eternal Life:
your Child, Jesus.

Remember your Church,
deliver it from evil,
and confirm it in your love.
Gather your Church from the four winds
into the Kingdom you have prepared.

Glory to you for ever!

EUCHARISTIC PRAYER FROM THE DIDACHE, (1ST-2ND CENTURY),
TRS. H. J. RICHARDS (B. 1921)

Peace and Calm?

The sermon annoyed me. Which was doubly frustrating, since I had deliberately gone to Mass on my own to have a quiet hour without the usual distractions.

It's not that I question the priest's right to interpret the Christian message. But what about my right? I've studied the Gospels too. Why is he allowed to monopolise the pulpit week after week?

He was talking about preparing for Christmas. All our rushing about, our shopping and planning of special meals, our worries over choosing presents, our paper chains and tinsel, our frantic last minute sending of cards – all this was worldly and contrary to the spirit of Christmas. Christmas, he said, is about the quiet coming of Christ into the world. We can only recognise it in peace and stillness.

At this point I wanted to stand up and shout, 'Objection!' God only present in peace and calm? Surely the whole Christmas story is about God being present everywhere, especially in the most ordinary events of life. Certainly the ordinary event of the birth of a baby is not a calm and still experience. Ask the women who have been through it.

CLARE RICHARDS (B. 1938)

A Son is Born

Do you want to know what goes on at the heart of the Trinity?
I'll tell you.
At the heart of the Trinity,
the Father laughs, and gives birth to the Son.
The Son then laughs back at the Father,
and gives birth to the Spirit.
Then the whole Trinity laughs,
and gives birth to us.

MEISTER ECKHART O. P. (1260-1327)

4 EMMANUEL: GOD WITH US

Scripture Readings

Take comfort, my people, take comfort –
it is the voice of your God –
bid Jerusalem be of good heart,
and tell her she has completed her prison sentence
and paid her penalty in full.

Listen! A voice is crying out:
'Make a road through the wilderness for the Lord,
cut a highway across the desert for our God,
fill in the valleys and level the hills,
straighten the bends and pave the rough ground,
so that the glory of the Lord may be seen by all,
and all people behold what the Lord has decreed.'

All humanity is grass, lasting no longer than wild flowers:
the grass withers and flowers fade
as soon as God's wind blows on them.
But the word of our God stands for ever.

Messenger, go to the top of the hill;
herald, shout as loud as you can,
and proclaim to the towns of Judah,
'Here is your God.'

BOOK OF ISAIAH 40:1-9

In him we knew a fullness never known before,
in him we saw a man fully living.

In him we see the God who can't be seen;
in him all things that will be or have been
have roots and take their being.

The universe, and all its millions teeming,
seen and unseen, in him find their meaning,
their reason and their value.

He lives in those who, breathing with his breath,
source of their life, and conqu'ror of their death,
together form his body.

St Paul to the Colossians 1:15-19

There has never been a time
when God has not told people that he loves them.
Right from the beginning,
and through all the ages,
that is what he has told all people everywhere.

But not all people have understood
what God was telling them,
even when God was saying, in so many words:
'Come and be members of my family.'

So this Word of God became a human being
and lived a human life like ours,
so that we could touch and feel what God was telling us.
The Word was made flesh and dwelt amongst us.
In him we see the God who can't be seen.
In him we see that God loves us.

Gospel of St John 1:1-18

The Descent of God

Let all mortal flesh keep silence,
and with fear and trembling stand,
ponder nothing earthly-minded,
for with blessing in his hand,
Christ our God to earth descendeth,
our full homage to demand.

King of kings, yet born of Mary,
as of old on earth he stood,
Lord of lords in human vesture,
in the body and the blood;
he will give to all the faithful
his own self for heavenly food.

Rank on rank the host of heaven
spreads its vanguard on the way,
as the Light of light descendeth
from the realms of endless day,
that the powers of hell may vanish
as the darkness clears away.

At his feet the six-winged Seraph;
Cherubim with sleepless eye
veil their faces to the presence,
as with ceaseless voice they cry:
Alleluia, Alleluia,
Alleluia, Lord most high.

4TH CENTURY LITURGY OF ST JAMES,
TRS. GERARD MOULTRIE (1829-1864)

Here is Your God

We proclaim to you, full of joy: Here is your God. This is the day that our Saviour is born, Christ the Lord.

A Saviour as a child, a Saviour as vulnerable, as inconspicuous and as unarmed as a child. A new-born baby cannot attack, cannot threaten, cannot kill. A baby reveals to me what all today's violence and war makes me forget. A baby calls the deepest, forgotten experiences back to me – that I am not a murderer, that I was not born to hate and kill.

Sometimes it seems to me as though the whole world is trying to persuade me to accept the law of the strongest, trying to convince me that aggression is good, that I must always be on my guard. But a child tells us that in the beginning it was not so. A new-born baby, that is, you shall not kill. He rescues us. He tells us that we are not murderers, we helmeted and masked men with our mortal fear of losing, turning our eyes fearfully away from almost every other man to avoid meeting his eyes. Yet we are good enough, all the same, to bring a child into the world, to look at him and to make him live. Christmas is not a man, not a hero, nothing to overwhelm us, but just a child – a child too little to cry out and protest against.

Here is your God. Nothing spectacular is taking place today. No extra session in Parliament. No sudden decision to devote two per cent of the gross national product to aid the developing countries. No voice calling 'Light' and there is light, 'Peace' and there is peace. No, that way does not exist. That God does not exist.

But God does exist. He happens in people who want to be so little that they are no longer able to kill. They follow, in themselves, the lonely way from war to peace. They beat their weapons into something quite ordinary, into a ploughshare for tilling the soil, a spoon for ladling up food. And they no longer train for battle.

He can happen in you. I hardly dare to say this, because it is so difficult, because the meaning in your life is the most difficult thing in your life. Beating your weapons – that happens in fire. But whoever recognizes this vision of peace recognizes his own future. It will happen – the wolf and the lamb will lie down together, the pitiless and the defenceless will be reconciled in us. It has been promised.

Huub Oosterhuis

Be You Our Redeemer, Lord

Rabbi Yochanan (1st century AD) said, 'A man was walking on a road at night, and his lantern went out. He lighted it, but it went out again. Finally he said to himself, "Why should I bother with the lantern? I will sit down at the roadside, and when the sunlight arrives, I will continue my journey."

By the same token, the Children of Israel were enslaved in Egypt, and Moses led them forth; they were enslaved in Babylon, and Zerubbabel led them forth; they were enslaved in Persia, and Mordecai led them forth; they were enslaved in Greece, and the Maccabees freed them. When they were enslaved once more by Rome, they said: "O Lord, free us no longer through the intervention of a man; we are weary of the succession of enslavement, freedom and enslavement. Be you our Redeemer, Lord, not a mortal man. Let not a man lighten us, but lighten us yourself, as it is written: With you is the fountain of Life, and in your Light do we see light."' *(Psalm 36:10)*

FROM THE MIDRASH ON THE PSALMS

God Was Man

And is it true? And is it true,
   This most tremendous tale of all,
Seen in a stained-glass window's hue,
   A Baby in an ox's stall?
The Maker of the stars and sea
Become a Child on earth for me?

And is it true? For if it is,
   No loving fingers tying strings
Around those tissued fripperies,
   The sweet and silly Christmas things,
Bath salts and inexpensive scent,
And hideous tie so kindly meant,

No love that in a family dwells,
   No carolling in frosty air,
Nor all the steeple-shaking bells
   Can with this single Truth compare –
That God was Man in Palestine
And lives to-day in Bread and Wine.

CHRISTMAS BY JOHN BETJEMAN (1906-1984)

God's Messenger

The Almighty himself, Creator of the universe,
the God whom no eye can discern,
has sent down from heaven his very own Truth,
  his holy Word,
to be planted in the heart of the human race.

To do this, one might have imagined he would send
some servant, some angel, some prince.
But no. He has sent
the very Artificer and Constructor of the universe,
through whom the heavens were made,
and the seas set within their bounds,
whose word is obeyed by the very elements of creation,
who assigns the sun the limits of its course by day,
and commands the moon to unveil its beams by night,
and orders the obedient stars to circle the heavens.
He is the Ordainer, Disposer and Ruler of all things,
of all that is in heaven and earth,
of the seas and all that they contain,
of fire, and air, and the deep,
of all that is above and below and in between.
Such is the Messenger God sent to the human race.

One might have imagined that his coming
would be in power, terror and awesomeness.
But no. His coming was in gentleness and humility.
God sent him as a king might send his own son,
and he came among us as a fellow human being.
For God would save us by persuasion, not by compulsion,
(there is no compulsion to be found in God)
and he sent him not to judge us, but out of love.

THE ANONYMOUS EPISTLE TO DIOGNETUS (2ND CENTURY)
TRS. H. J. RICHARDS (B. 1921)

Incarnation

When I go from hence
let this be my parting word:
that what I have seen is unsurpassable.

I have tasted of the hidden honey of this lotus
that expands on the ocean of light,
and thus I am blessed –
let this be my parting word.

In this playhouse of infinite forms
I have had my play,
and here I have caught sight
of Him that is formless.

My whole body and my limbs have been thrilled
with His touch who is beyond touch;
and if the end comes here –
let this be my parting word.

RABINDRANATH TAGORE (1861-1941)

A New Idea of God

Jesus brings in a new idea of God. We do not know, in advance of Jesus, what God is like. Otherwise we would not call Jesus 'the Word of God'. We could dispense with his services.

Jesus does not simply corroborate the notions of the Greek philosophers. He tells us, or better, he *shows* us what God is like. God is Love and Forgiveness. The philosophers found these characteristics so alien to the deity that *they never thought of attributing them to God.* After Jesus, it isn't possible for Christians to picture God except as the merciful and all-forgiving Father of our Lord Jesus Christ who loves and justifies the sinner. All this helps to explain why Jesus is termed Emmanuel, God-with-us and God-for-us. He is our Way to God, a new way that does not depend on philosophical arguments . . .

Jesus brings in this strange, new idea of God: through those aspects of human life usually thought to be most distant from God – in fact, the challenge to the very existence of the deity: pain, failure, humiliation, death – the divine is manifest in Christ's own life, and thus mediated to us.

PETER DE ROSA (B. 1932)

Incarnate

Christ became a man of his people and of his time:
he lived as a Jew,
he worked as a labourer of Nazareth,
and since then he continues
to become incarnate in everyone.
If many have distanced themselves from the Church,
it is precisely because the Church
has often distanced itself from humanity.
But a Church that can feel as its own
all that is human,
and wants to incarnate the pain,
the hope,
the affliction of all who suffer and feel joy,
such a Church will be Christ loved and awaited,
Christ present.
And that depends on us.

OSCAR ROMERO (1917-1980)

God and Man

In the beginning
God made physicists
out of nothing at all.

'Now hold on'
said the physicists
'that's against a law'.

God,
having not yet made Newton,
said nothing.

Then God made theologians
and became man
and joined them.

'Oh no'
said the theologians
'it's one thing or the other,
God *or* man'.

God smiled
and passed the bread and wine.

GODFREY RUST

Flesh

The 'flesh' is the concrete person.
The flesh is we who are present here –
people just beginning to live,
the vigorous adolescent,
the old man nearing the end.
The flesh is marked by time.
The flesh is the actual human situation,
human beings in sin,
human beings in painful situations,
the people of a nation
that seems to have got into a blind alley.
The flesh is all of us who live incarnate.

And this flesh, this frail flesh
that has beginning and end,
that sickens and dies,
that becomes miserable or happy –
that is what the Word of God became.
The Word was made flesh.

OSCAR ROMERO (1917-1980)

Mid-Winter

In the bleak mid-winter,
frosty wind made moan,
earth stood hard as iron,
water like a stone;
snow had fallen, snow on snow,
snow on snow,
in the bleak mid-winter,
long ago.

Our God, heaven cannot hold him,
nor earth sustain;
heaven and earth shall flee away
when he comes to reign;
in the bleak mid-winter
a stable place sufficed
the Lord God almighty,
Jesus Christ.

Angels and archangels
may have gathered there,
cherubim and seraphim
thronged the air;
but his mother only,
in her maiden bliss,
worshipped the Belovèd
with a kiss.

What can I give him,
poor as I am?
If I were a shepherd,
I would bring a lamb;
if I were a wise man,
I would do my part;
yet what can I give him –
give my heart.

CHRISTINA GEORGINA ROSSETTI (1830-1894)

5 TODAY

Scripture Readings

For anyone who is in Christ
there is a new creation;
the old order is gone
and a new one is here.

ST PAUL TO THE CORINTHIANS (II) 5:17

God so loved the world
that he gave his only Son,
so that everyone who believes in him
may here and now have eternal life . . .
Anyone who believes in the Son
already has eternal life . . .
Believe me, the time is coming –
in fact it is here now –
when the dead hear the voice of the Son of God,
and hearing it, live . . .
Eternal life is this:
to know, now,
you, the one true God,
through the Christ whom you have sent.

GOSPEL OF JOHN 3:16, 3:36, 5:25, 17:3

Here, Not There

Father, the Christmas story tempts us
to turn our religion into an anachronism,
something that belongs to the past,
and we waste precious time wondering
how to bring it back into the present again.

Teach us that your Son is here, not there.
Remind us that the gospel is in the fact of Christ,
not in his setting;
and that the story of his birth
does not add up to very much
without the story of his claims and his deeds,
his death and his disciples.

Father, you have brought us here together
on the strength of some vision of your glory already seen;
and in this we are not so unlike the shepherds.
Help us, then, so to approach Bethlehem
that our vision may be verified for us,
as theirs was for them.
May we, too, become part of the story of Christ's life.
We ask this in his name.

CONTEMPORARY PRAYERS, ED. CARYL MICKLEM (B. 1925)

Born Today

Come, all you unbelieving men,
I'm glad to see you today:
I'll tell you of a miracle
two thousand years away

> We can't believe in a miracle
> two thousand years away
> but only in a miracle
> that we can see today.

The shepherds came to a cattle shed
two thousand years away,
and there they found the Son of God
a-lying in the hay.

> We can't believe in a Son of God
> two thousand years away
> but only in a Son of God
> that we can see today.

They won't believe in the Bible now,
they want to touch and see;
but Matthew, Mark and Luke and John
were good enough for me.

> They're good enough for the Pope of Rome,
> and Billy Graham and you,
> but you can't believe what you can't believe
> so what are we to do?

Christ was born in a cattle shed
two thousand years away,
but still he can be born again
in you and me today.

> Show us where the Son of God
> is being born today.

SYDNEY CARTER (B. 1915)

Living Now

Your holy hearsay
is not evidence;
give me the good news
in the present tense.
What happened
nineteen hundred years ago
may not have happened –
how am I to know?

The living truth
is what I long to see;
I cannot lean upon
what used to be.
So shut the Bible up
and tell me how
the Christ you talk about
is living now.

SYDNEY CARTER (B. 1915)

Christmas in Prison

From the Christian point of view there is no special problem about Christmas in a prison cell. For many people in this building it will probably be a more sincere and genuine occasion than in places where nothing but the name is kept. That misery, suffering, poverty, loneliness, helplessness, and guilt mean something quite different in the eyes of God from what they mean in the judgement of man, that God will approach where men turn away, that Christ was born in a stable because there was no room for him in the inn – these are things that a prisoner can understand better than other people; for him they really are glad tidings, and that faith gives him a part in the communion of saints, a Christian fellowship breaking the bounds of time and space and reducing the months of confinement here to insignificance.

DIETRICH BONHOEFFER (1906-1945)

Christ Present

O world invisible, we view thee,
O world intangible, we touch thee,
O world unknowable, we know thee,
inapprehensible, we clutch thee!

Does the fish soar to find the ocean,
the eagle plunge to find the air –
that we ask of the stars in motion
if they have rumour of thee there?

Not where the wheeling systems darken,
and our benumbed conceiving soars! –
The drift of pinions, would we hearken,
beats at our own clay-shuttered doors.

The angels keep their ancient places; –
turn but a stone, and start a wing!
'Tis ye, 'tis your estrangèd faces,
that miss the many-splendoured thing.

But (when so sad thou canst not sadder)
cry; – and upon thy so sore loss
shall shine the traffic of Jacob's ladder
pitched betwixt Heaven and Charing Cross.

Yea, in the night, my soul, my daughter,
cry, – clinging Heaven by the hems;
and lo, Christ walking on the water
not of Gennesareth, but Thames!

FRANCIS THOMPSON (1859-1907)

If He Comes Not Now

If he comes not now,
what if two thousand years ago he came?
He will not notice when my head I bow,
if he comes not now;
he will not hear me when I speak his name,
if he comes not now.

If he comes at death,
if only at that hour he whispers, 'Look!
I am here to receive your last faint breath',
if he comes at death,
today I will not find him in a Book,
if he comes not now.

If he comes for me,
must he not come for me throughout each day,
and in the nights when I no longer see?
If he comes for me,
will he not say, 'You have not lost the way',
if he comes for me?

PETER DE ROSA (B. 1932)

Such An Ordinary Man

I saw myself, in a dream, a youth, almost a boy, in a low-pitched wooden church. The slim wax candles gleamed, spots of red, before the old pictures of the saints.

A ring of coloured light encircled each tiny flame. Dark and dim it was in the church, which was full of people. All fair-haired, peasant heads. From time to time they began swaying, falling, rising again, like the ripe ears of wheat, when the wind of summer passes in slow undulation over them.

All at once some man came up from behind and stood beside me.

I did not turn towards him; but at once I felt that this man was Christ.

Emotion, curiosity, awe overmastered me suddenly. I made an effort, and looked at my neighbour.

A face like everyone's, a face like all men's faces. The eyes looked a little upwards, quietly and intently. The lips closed, but not compressed; the upper lip, as it were, resting on the lower; a small beard parted in two. The hands folded and still. And the clothes on him like everyone's.

'What sort of Christ is this?' I thought. 'Such an ordinary, ordinary man! It can't be! . . .'

And then my heart sank, and I came to myself, and realized that just such a face – a face like all men's faces – is the face of Christ.

IVAN SERGEYEVITCH TURGENEV
(1818-1883)

Today

From tomorrow on I shall be sad,
from tomorrow on.
Not today. Today I will be glad.

And every day,
no matter how bitter it may be,
I shall say;
From tomorrow on I shall be sad,
not today.

AN ANONYMOUS CHILD IN A NAZI DEATH CAMP.

I Do Confess Thee Here

One of the crowd went up,
And knelt before the Paten and the Cup,
Received the Lord, returned in peace, and prayed
Close to my side. Then in my heart I said:

O Christ, in this man's life –
This stranger who is Thine – in all his strife,
All his felicity, his good and ill,
In the assaulted stronghold of his will,

I do confess Thee here
Alive within this life; I know Thee near
Within this lowly conscience, closed away,
Within this brother's solitary day,

Christ in his unknown heart,
His intellect unknown – this love, this art,
This battle and this peace, this destiny,
That I shall never know, look upon me!

Christ in his numbered breath,
Christ in his beating heart and in his death,
Christ in his mystery! From that secret place
And from that separate dwelling, give me grace.

ALICE MEYNELL (1847-1922)

He Comes To Meet Me

Even if Jesus of Nazareth is not all that many of you Christians hold him to be, he is nonetheless, for me too, for me as a Jew, a central figure whom I cannot exclude from my life . . . The further I have gone along the road of life, the nearer I have come to the figure of Jesus.

At every turning of the road he has been standing, repeatedly putting the question he asked at Caesarea Philippi, 'Who am I?' And repeatedly I have had to give him an answer.

And I am convinced that he will continue to go with me, as long as I go along my road, and that he will constantly come to meet me as he once came to meet Peter on the Via Appia, so legend tells us, and as he once came to meet Paul, as the Acts of the Apostles relate, on the Damascus Road.

Again and again I meet him, and again and again we converse together on the basis of our common Jewish origins and of Jewish hopes for the coming Kingdom. And since I left Christian Europe and went to live in Jewish Israel, he has come closer to me. For I am now living in his land and among his people, and his sayings and parables are as close and as alive for me, as though it was all happening here and now. When at the Passover meal I lift the cup and break the unleavened bread, I am doing what he did, and I know that I am much closer to him than many Christians who celebrate the Eucharist in complete separation from its Jewish origins.

SHALOM BEN-CHORIN

6 TOMORROW

Scripture Readings

Bless'd be the God whom Jesus called Father:
to him be glory and praise.

In Christ we are already in heaven;
in Christ, before the world began,
God chose us as his holy people,
as the sisters and brothers of Christ;
  This was the gracious purpose of God;
  to him be glory and praise.

In Christ, God's plan is laid open;
in Christ, time has come to an end;
for all things, on earth and in heaven,
are to be made whole in Christ.
  This was the gracious purpose of God;
  to him be glory and praise.

In Christ, the God who guides all things,
who rules all events and all time,
chose one out of all of the nations
as the first to hope for Christ.
  This was the gracious purpose of God;
  to him be glory and praise.

In Christ, this good news of salvation
has spread to the nations of the world;
they too have received Christ's Spirit
as the pledge that heaven is theirs.
  This was the gracious purpose of God;
  to him be glory and praise.

The Body of Christ is being built up.
We shall all at last reach unity
in the faith and knowledge of the Son of God
and form the Perfect Man . . .
If we live by the truth, and in love,
we shall grow completely into Christ.
That is how the Body grows
until it has built itself up in love.

EPISTLE TO THE EPHESIANS 1:3-14, 4:12-16

Love Received and Love Given

The times are difficult.
They call for courage and faith.
Faith is in the end a lonely virtue.
Lonely especially where a deeply authentic community of love
is not an accomplished fact,
but a job to be begun over and over,
as in all Christian communities in general.
Love is not something we get from Mother Church
as a child gets milk from the breast;
it also has to be given.
We don't get any love if we don't give any . . .
Christmas is not then just a sweet regression
to breast feeding and infancy.
It is a serious and sometimes difficult feast.
Difficult especially if for psychological reasons
we fail to grasp the indestructible kernel of hope that is in it.
If we are just looking for a little consolation
we may be disappointed.
Let us pray for one another,
love one another in truth,
in the sobriety of earnest Christian hope,
for hope, says Paul,
does not deceive.

THOMAS MERTON (1915-1968)

This is True

It is not true
that this world and its people
are doomed to die and be lost.
    This is true:
    God so loved the world
    that he gave his only begotten Son,
    that whosoever believes in him,
    shall not perish but have everlasting life.

It is not true
that we must accept inhumanity and discrimination,
hunger and poverty, death and destruction.
    This is true:
    I have come that they may have life,
    and that abundantly.

It is not true
that violence and hatred should have the last word,
and that war and destruction have come to stay for ever.
    This is true:
    Unto us a child is born,
    and unto us a Son is given,
    and the government shall be upon his shoulder,
    and his name shall be called
    Wonderful Counsellor, Mighty God,
    the Everlasting Father, the Prince of Peace.

ALLAN BOESAK (B. 1945)

Christmas and Easter

Christmas is really
for the children.
Especially for children
who like animals, stables,
stars and babies wrapped
in swaddling clothes.
Then there are wise men,
kings in fine robes,
humble shepherds and a
hint of rich perfume.

Easter is not really
for the children
unless accompanied by a
cream filled egg.
It has whips, blood, nails,
a spear and allegations
of body snatching.
It involves politics, God
and the sins of the world.
It is not good for people
of a nervous disposition.
They would do better to
think on rabbits, chickens
and the first snowdrop
of spring.
Or they'd do better to
wait for a re-run of
Christmas without asking
too many questions about
what Jesus did when he grew up
or whether there's any connection.

STEVE TURNER

The Hidden Jesus

There are people after Jesus.
They have seen the signs.
Quick, let's hide him.

Let's think: carpenter,
    fishermen's friend,
      disturber of religious comfort.
Let's award him a degree in theology,
a purple cassock
and a position of respect.
They'll never think of looking there.

Let's think: his dialect may betray him,
    his tongue is of the masses.
Let's teach him Latin
and seventeenth century English.
They'll never think of listening in.

Let's think: humble,
    Man of Sorrows,
      nowhere to lay his head.
We'll build a house for him,
somewhere away from the poor.
We'll fill it with brass and silence.
It's sure to throw them off.

There are people after Jesus.
Quick, let's hide him.

STEVE TURNER

Simple Message

We are forced to note the extreme simplicity of the message of Jesus. An old era is done. God is intervening to begin a new age. It is an era of incredible generosity. One must change one's life in order to benefit from the generosity, but so great is the payoff in accepting the abundance of the new age that our *metanoia* ought to be one not of sorrow and sacrifice but of wonder and rejoicing.

This message speaks to the most fundamental questions one can ask: Is reality malign or gracious? Jesus replies that it is gracious to the point of insane generosity. Is life absurd or does it have a purpose? The reply of Jesus is that not only does it have purpose but that God has directly intervened in human events to make it perfectly clear what the purpose is. What is the nature of the Really Real? Jesus' response is that the Really Real is generous, forgiving, saving love. How does a good man behave? The good man is a person who is captivated by the joy and wonder of God's promise. In the end, will life triumph over death or death over life? Jesus is perfectly confident: the Kingdom of his Father cannot be vanquished, not even by death . . .

The message of Jesus, the Good News of the Kingdom of his Father, deserves to be accepted or rejected for what it is: an answer to *the* most fundamental questions we could ask. If we are to reject it, then let us reject it because we believe that evil triumphs over good, that life is absurd and is a tale told by an idiot, that the Really Real is malign, and that only a blind fool would believe that things will be alright in the end. For it is on this ground that we must accept or reject Jesus, not on matters of papal infallibility or the virgin birth, or the stupidity of ecclesiastical leaders, or the existence of angels, or whether the Church has anything relevant to say about social reform.

ANDREW GREELEY (B. 1928)

Birth or Death?

A cold coming we had of it,
just the worst time of the year
for a journey, and such a long journey:
the ways deep and the weather sharp,
the very dead of winter.
And the camels galled, sore-footed, refractory,
lying down in the melting snow.
There were times we regretted
the summer palaces on slopes, the terraces,
and the silken girls bringing sherbet.
Then the camel men cursing and grumbling
and running away, and wanting their liquor and women,
and the night-fires going out, and the lack of shelters,
and the cities hostile and the towns unfriendly
and the villages dirty and charging high prices:
a hard time we had of it.
At the end we preferred to travel all night,
sleeping in snatches,
with the voices singing in our ears, saying
that this was all folly

Then at dawn we came down to a temperate valley,
wet, below the snow line, smelling of vegetation;
with a running stream and a water-mill beating the darkness,
and three trees on a low sky,
and an old white horse galloped away in the meadow.
Then we came to a tavern with vine-leaves over the lintel,
six hands at an open door dicing for silver,
and feet kicking the empty wine-skins.
But there was no information, and so we continued
and arrived at evening, not a moment too soon
finding the place; it was (you may say) satisfactory.

All this was a long time ago, I remember,
and I would do it again, but set down
this set down
this: were we led all that way for
Birth or Death? There was a Birth, certainly,
we had evidence and no doubt. I had seen birth and death,
but had thought they were different; this Birth was
hard and bitter agony for us, like Death, our death.
We returned to our places, these Kingdoms,
but no longer at ease here, in the old dispensation,
with an alien people clutching their gods.
I should be glad of another death.

THE JOURNEY OF THE MAGI BY T. S. ELIOT (1888-1935)

Finish the Work

Don't wait for an angel, don't look for a star,
to tell you the message or guide you from far.
They're part of the background for art-lovers' eyes,
to help them to measure the portrait for size.
    He's only a baby to grow to a man:
    to call you to finish the work he began.

It isn't to Bethlehem shepherds must go,
but to look for the missing lamb under the snow.
It isn't on camels that real kings ride,
but on asses and crosses with robbers beside.
    He's only a baby to grow to a man:
    to call you to finish the work he began.

Now all you good people from bench and from sink,
come turn up the volume and hear yourselves think:
Who else on his birthday's put back in a cot?
Do you reckon Act One is as good as the lot?
    He's only a baby to grow to a man:
    to call you to finish the work he began.

CONTEMPORARY PRAYERS, ED. CARYL MICKLEM (B. 1925)

Why Christ Came

Thank God . . .
for empty churches
and bursting shops;
for the soldier's Christmas Eve patrol;
for starvation
and gluttony;
for reckless randy playboys;
for tenements
and prisons;
for apartheid-cheapened oranges;
for boring sermons
and trivial TV;
for minds warped by bent schooling;
for drunks
and thugs;
for wreaths made out of holly;
for mucked-up sex
and prudery;
for comfortable affluence;
for ignorance
and selfishness;
for foreigners in foreign lands;
for missiles
and war toys;
for hymns that can't be understood;
for me
and mine.

Thank God for these
else we would soon forget
the world to which Christ came
(and why)
and lose the meaning
in the cosy celebration.

DAVID J. HARDING (B. 1941)

7   A SELECTION OF COLLECTS

Advent

1   Almighty God,
     give us grace that we may cast away the works
        of darkness,
     and put upon us the armour of light,
     now in the time of this mortal life,
     in which thy Son Jesus Christ came to visit us
        in great humility;
     that in the last day,
     when he shall come again in his glorious Majesty
     to judge both the quick and the dead,
     we may rise to the life immortal,
     through him who liveth and reigneth with thee
        and the Holy Spirit,
     now and ever. Amen.

BOOK OF COMMON PRAYER

2   Lord our God,
     you are the God who has spoken,
     and mankind has taken ages
     to see the unfolding
     of your marvellous salvation history.
     You are the God who speaks,
     and also the God who is coming.
     Come, then, O Lord!
     Wait no longer!
     Come, in Jesus Christ, your Son –
     God made present,
     who lives and reigns with you and the Spirit
     in eternal bliss.

PIERRE GRIOLET

3   Lord, you wait for us
until we are open to you.
We wait for your word
to make us receptive.
Attune us to your voice,
to your silence,
speak and bring your Son to us –
Jesus, the word of your peace.

4   Your word is near,
O Lord our God,
your grace is near.
Come to us, then,
with mildness and power.
Do not let us be deaf to you,
but make us receptive and open
to Jesus Christ your Son,
who will come to look for us and save us
today and every day
for ever and ever.

5   You, God, arouse faith in our hearts,
whoever we are.
You know and accept all your people,
whatever their thoughts are of you.
Speak to the world, then, your word;
come with your heaven among us;
shine your sun on good and bad alike.

6   Grant us, O Lord,
a sign of life.
Show us, O God,
how much we mean to you.
Come into our world
with your word of creation.
Make us fit to receive you
and grant us your peace.

7   O Lord, our God,
    you give your light, your word
    to all who want it.
    You give your Kingdom
    to the poor and the sinners.
    Then why not give your grace
    to us as well?
    Do not send us away
    emptyhanded,
    but fill us with your Son,
    your word,
    the light and life of the world
    for all ages.

8   It is your word,
    it is Jesus Christ
    that we are aiming at, Lord God.
    Whom else should we
    expect from you?
    He is your heart, your Son,
    your pity;
    He is your eyes and has seen us,
    he is your mouth and speaks to us,
    and we know and receive you
    in his words.
    We ask you, Lord,
    to let us see this man,
    knowing that who sees him
    beholds you, the Father,
    and this is enough
    for us as for this world
    and for all times. Amen.

9   O God, your name
has been with us on earth
from the beginning,
a word so full of promise
that it has kept us going.
But in the life of Jesus
You have revealed your name.
You, our Father, can be found
in him for all time.
He is your word and promise
completely.
We ask you that we may
be drawn to him
and thereby come
to know you more and more.

10   God and Father of Jesus Christ,
confirm and strengthen our belief
that it is he whom we expect,
and that in him your light
has shone upon the world.
We pray to you,
take from us everything
that cannot bear this light
and make us love your peace.
Amen.

11   Lord God,
as a miracle of humanity and love,
as a word that makes people free,
your Son has come to us,
and where he comes
life is no longer dark and fearful.
We pray that he
may come to life among us here,
that we may not be ensnared in confusion,
obsessed with doubt and discord,
but that we may be filled
with faith and courage,
simplicity and peace.

HUUB OOSTERHUIS

Christmas

1   Our Father in heaven,
you have lit up this most holy night
with the brightness of Christ,
the Light of the World.
His light has already shone on us
in all the sacraments we celebrate.
Bring us to that heaven
where his light shines for ever and ever.

ROMAN MISSAL,
TRS. H. J. RICHARDS (B. 1921)

2   Lord Jesus Christ,
you have forgiven us
for being as we are –
people with love and hatred
in our hearts,
with a plank in our eyes
and words of stone in our mouths.
You came to us
to be human like ourselves,
to become sin.
At your wits' end
and for all eternity,
you do not know
what more you can do
than to treat people,
every person,
as more important than yourself.
I am that person.

3   You, God, are not
    as we think you are.
    You have shown us
    that you are different
    in Jesus Christ, your Son,
    light of your light
    who humbly trod the path
    that anyone treads in this world,
    and this is how you saved us.
    We thank you
    for coming to us
    and for being so close to us
    in this man, Jesus,
    today and every day.

4   We thank you, holy Father,
    Lord our God,
    for Jesus your beloved Son
    whom you called and sent
    to serve us and give us light,
    to bring your Kingdom
    to the poor,
    to bring redemption
    to all captive people,
    and to be for ever
    and for all mankind
    the likeness and the form
    of your constant love and goodness.
    We thank you
    for this unforgettable man
    who has fulfilled everything
    that is human –
    our life and death.
    We thank you
    because he gave himself,
    heart and soul, to this world.

HUUB OOSTERHUIS

ACKNOWLEDGEMENTS

All the scripture readings in this anthology are translations by H. J. Richards, © copyright 1994 by Kevin Mayhew Ltd.

The publishers wish to express their gratitude to the following for permission to reproduce copyright material in this publication:

The Revd. James Badcock for *A Dissenter's Hail Mary* from 'Flowing Streams', published by NCEC.

Nadine Brummer for *Jewish Madonna*.

Burns & Oates Ltd, Wellwood, North Farm Road, Tunbridge Wells, Kent TN2 3DR for *Virgin Mother* translated by R. A. Knox. Also for *He Comes to Meet Me* by Shalom Ben-Chorin from 'The Church'.

Church House Publishing, Church House, Great Smith Street, London SW1P 3NZ for *It is not true* by Allan Boesak from 'Voices from Vancouver'.

Church Missionary Society, Partnership House, 157 Waterloo Road, London SE1 8UU for *Trembling Expectancy* (Advent) by Chandran Devanesen from 'Morning, Noon and Night'.

Peter De Rosa for *The Slave of the Lord* from 'A Bible Prayer-Book for Today', Fontana 1976, *A New Idea of God* from 'Jesus Who Became Christ', Collins 1975, and *If He Comes Not Now*.

Faber & Faber Ltd, 3 Queen Square, London WC1N 3AU for *The Cultivation of Christmas Trees* and *The Journey of the Magi* from 'Collected Poems 1909-1962' by T. S. Eliot.

HarperCollins Publishers, 77-85 Fulham Palace Road, Hammersmith, London W6 8JB for *This Is What Advent Is, Incarnate* and *Flesh* from 'The Violence of Love, The Pastoral Wisdom of Archbishop Oscar Romero', edited and translated by James Brickman.

Hodder & Stoughton Ltd, 338 Euston Road, London NW1 3BH for *Christmas and Easter* and *The Hidden Jesus* from 'Up to Date' by Steve Turner.

McCrimmon Publishing Co Ltd, 10-12 High Street, Great Wakering, Southend-on-Sea, Essex SS3 OEQ for *Come, Lord Jesus* from 'Pilgrim to the Holy Land' by Donald Hilton.

Thomas Merton Legacy Trust, New York for *Love Received and Love Given* (Christmas Letter) © Trustees of the Merton Legacy Trust.

John Murray (Publishers) Ltd, 50 Albermarle Street, London W1X 4BD for *Christmas* by John Betjeman from 'Collected Poems'.

National Christian Education Council, Robert Denholm House, Nutfield, Redhill, Surrey RH1 4HW for *God So Loved* by W. S. Beattie, *Don't Wait for an Angel* by Caryl Micklem and *Why Christ Came* by David J. Harding from 'A Word in Season'. Also *Lord of Surprises* by Donald Hilton from 'Prayers for the Church Community'.

Paulist Press, 997 Macarthur Blvd, Mahwah, NJ 07430, USA for *Till He Comes* and *Lord our God* from 'You Call Us Together' by Pierre Griolet.

Reform Synagogues of Gt Britain, The Manor House, 80 East End Road, Finchley, London N3 25Y for *Thy Kingdom Come, Today I am Coming* and *Be You Our Redeemer, Lord* from 'Forms of Prayer for Jewish Worship, Vol 1, Daily & Sabbath Prayerbook', Reform Synagogues of Gt Britain, London, 1977.

SCM Press Ltd, 26-30 Tottenham Road, London N1 4BZ for *The God Who Comes* and *Here, Not There* from 'Contemporary Prayers for Public Worship', ed. Caryl Micklem, SCM Press 1967. Also for *For a Christian there is nothing* from 'Letters and Papers from Prison, the Enlarged Edition' by Dietrich Bonhoeffer, SCM Press 1971.

Sheed & Ward Ltd, 14 Cooper's Row, London EC3N 2BH for *Here is Your God* by Huub Ooesterhuis from 'Prayers, Poems and Songs'.

Ted Schmidt for *A New Future, Liberty for Captives* and *The Unspeakable New.* SPCK, Holy Trinity Church, Marylebone Road, London NW1 4DU for *The Messiah Comes* from 'Praying with the Jewish Tradition', translated by Paula Clifford (SPCK 1988).

Stainer & Bell Ltd, PO Box 110, Victoria House, 23 Gruneisen Road, Finchley, London N3 1DZ for *I Carry the Maker of the World, Two Thousand Years Away* and *Your Holy Hearsay* by Sydney Carter.

Vallentine Mitchell Publishers, Newbury House, 890-900 Eastern Avenue, Newbury Park, Ilford, Essex IG2 7HH for *It Will All Come Right* by Anne Frank from 'The Diary of Anne Frank'.

Copyright Control: *Simple Message* by Andrew Greeley, *In Thy Coming* by Eric Milner-White, *God and Man* by Godfrey Rust and *Lord, you wait for us, O Lord, our God, O God, your name, You, God, are not as we think* and *Lord Jesus Christ* by Huub Ooesterhuis.